# How to train kittens

Tips and techniques for raising
happy and well-behaved kittens"
Copyright 2023
By ab Ahmad

## Contents

**Introduction**

Training your kitten is an essential part of raising a happy and well-behaved pet. In addition to assisting you in avoiding problematic behaviors, training also improves your relationship with your pet. However, training a kitten can be challenging due to their distinct personalities and short attention spans. In this guide, we will show you how to train your kitten, from teaching basic obedience to socialization and teaching how to use the litter box. By following these guidelines, you can assist your kitten in becoming a well-behaved and adored member of your family.

## Chapter 1

### Kitten Training Tips

The process of preparing your young cat can be amusing as well as profitable for both of you. Here are around fifteen suggestions to help you prepare your cat:

(1) Start exercising earlier than planned: Preparation should begin as soon as time permits when your cat is between the ages of 8 and 12 weeks.

(2) Appreciation for appropriate behavior: When your kitten behaves well, reward it with treats, toys, and praise. If you shout or respond with a rebuke, you might feel fear and anxiety.

(3) Do as instructed: When preparing your kitten, use the same commands and rewards each time.

(4) Limit the number of instructional meetings: Felines should have brief, consistent educational meetings, preferably lasting 5 to 10 minutes a few times per day.

5. Make use of a clicker: A clicker is a useful tool for recognizing correct behavior and letting you know when your cat has figured something out.

(6) Make smart use of treats: Treats can be given to your cat as a reward for good behavior, but they should not be used to reward or overindulge it.

(7) Instruct fundamental orders: Learn the essential commands "sit," "remain," "come," and "down" for your cat.

(8) Introduce your cat to other people: Introduce your kitten to new people, animals, and environments to help them become more sociable and balanced.

9) Teach proper scratching techniques: When you set one up for your small cat, encourage them to use it instead of your furniture.

10) Preparing using a litter box: To encourage your kitten to use the litter box, show them where it is. Clean and effectively open the litter box.

11) Use your intuition when playing with toys: Playing with toys will get your young cat moving, holding, and stimulated intellectually.

(12) Make use of a rope and tackle: For safe outdoor exploration, train your cat to walk on a chain and outfit.

13. Make use of a transporter: You can make it easier for your young cat to leave the house and go to the vet by making them feel safe and secure in a transporter.

(14). Establish points of no return: Determine what your kitten should and shouldn't do, such as not jumping on ledges or scratching people.

(15) Have a good time and act restrained: Keep in mind that getting your kitten ready takes time, patience, and perseverance. Take in as much as you can, and take pleasure in watching your kitten grow and learn! Keep in mind that getting your kitten ready should be fun for you both. Enjoy it, be patient, and take pleasure in watching your kitten grow and learn!

# The Seven Most Crucial Methods of Cat Training Your Cat Can Actually Learn

Contrary to popular belief, training cats is just as enjoyable! Cat training is a great way to get to know your cat and teach her important words. I dare say that training cats is just as enjoyable as training dogs, as an equal opportunity pet enthusiast. When the lessons are accompanied by entertainment and food, most kittens also respond well to leash training. Your cat will appreciate you learning the basics. As the director of Jones Animal Behavior in Rhode Island, behaviorist Katenna Jones, ACAAB, asserts, "Many cats love training if done correctly, with patience, and with rewards." You only get what you put into a relationship, just like in any other one!

Dogs are bred to perform a wide range of tasks, whereas cats are naturally taught the basics. Cats will instinctively use a litter box, and it's simple to avoid common dog behaviors like biting in play.

A common method for training a cat not to bite or pull on a leash is to avoid initiating the behavior in the first place.

When teaching your cat to walk on a leash, don't use a training collar because it can cause your cat to choke and activate a frantic oppositional reflex. Redirect your cat's predatory instincts to a feathery toy to teach her not to bite if she does. Training cats has numerous advantages. Jones asserts that training fosters positive social contact in addition to providing mental and physical stimulation. Independent training can be very beneficial for cats who are irritable, bored, shy, or afraid. Walk for a minute in your cat's paws before beginning your project on training her. Behaviorist Stanley Coren, PhD, DSc, FRSC, claims that unlike dogs, cats interact with their families more like toddlers do. Cats are motivated by pay-to-play incentives, whereas dogs will cooperate in exchange for a few kind words. Cats will only participate in training games if the rewards are worthwhile, despite our exuberant enthusiasm.

## There are seven abilities your cat can use

Cat training is a wonderful method for establishing a connection with your cat and teaching them the meanings of important words. The most important thing is to let your cat decide what you teach them. According to Ingrid Johnson, CCBC and director of Fundamentally Feline in Georgia, "Not all cats like to do all things." Before attempting to teach your cat new behaviors, choose those that it already carries out on its own.

She adds, "Keep it positive." Clicker training is an extremely efficient method for determining when your cat exhibits the desired behavior.

Simply verbalizing and rewarding your cat's natural behaviors is the essence of cat training.

There are seven methods for teaching your cat to speak and behave:

## 1. Gentle

Always use your hands to reward your cats. To stop biting, dab some treat paste—whether homemade or purchased at a store—on your knuckles or the back of your hand. When your cat or kitten starts to nip or bite, say "gentle" and gently pull your hand away from her.

## 2. Confirm It

When your cat is able to follow the treats, add the phrase "Find It" to them. Yes, it's that simple. The shell game can then be played with the Tupperware containers or even with your hands. Apply cat paste to the area where she bites or claws at your hand after you say "gentle." Show her the treat whenever she licks or taps your hand gently with her paw.

## 3. Target

You can use either a homemade or store-bought point of your finger, or both. You can get your cat to notice the object by placing it two inches in front of its nose. You can click to reward her when she touches it. To indicate your cat's consistent movement toward the target, use the word "target."

## 4. Sit

When your cat sits naturally, reward her with a click and a treat. Your cat will soon sit to cue you when you bring out the treats. Include the word "sit" once you can predict her behavior. Then, try directing her there with a target wand or pointing signal. Click it to reward this pose. Utilizing the clicker and treats on occasion will reduce the number of correct clicks to one. Using intermittent rewards as a teaching strategy is more effective because Kitty is more likely to perform when she does not know when she will receive a reward.

## 5. Hold onto your mat tightly

To make a cat mat, place a flat mat, towel, or cloth napkin on the counter, sofa, or tabletop. Her curiosity will not kill her, but it will control her! When she steps onto the mat, click. After that, you'll have to throw a treat a little way from the mat to get your cat to come back for the next round. Use the prompt "on your mat" to maintain consistency in your presence. When your cat goes to her mat willingly and stays there, give her the "stay" command. You can get your cat to stay in a place like her cat tree while you eat or cook with her by using the mat. Your cat-mat can also be taken on vacation or to the vet to help calm your cat during checkups.

## 6. Come

A cat can learn to come when it first enters your home. The act of shaking a treat cup and positive experiences ought to go hand in hand with the word "come." In a cup or other container, you can shake treats until your cat hears them. Click on your cat and give her a treat when she arrives. Increase the amount of time between saying "come" and shaking the treats gradually until she arrives on time. Reward her from time to time as you gradually remove the clicker.

## 7. The carrier or box for the cat:

Most cats like to look inside a box or bag. A strategy for dealing with this behavior is helpful when it comes time to remove the cat carrier. In fact, the cat carrier can be used to store treats and even feed portions of food to your cat or kitten long before you need them. Every time your cat enters a carrier or box, give it praise and click on it. When your cat calls to you, whenever you can, include the cue "in the box." As a means of rewarding her for each ride, gradually transporting her in her box or carrier.

Because they frequently necessitate a great deal of concentration, lessons that last less than five minutes are ideal. Have some fun at the end of each game with a feather flyer or stuffed toy and let your cat win.

## How to Place Your Cat in a Carryall: Advice from a Pro

You can teach your cat to love her carrier at home or on the go with these tips. We are also guided through a straightforward two-step procedure for placing your cat in her crate by a specialist in fearless training.

At the Toronto Humane Society, Shannen McNee, a Certified Cat Behavior Consultant and specialist in fear-free training, taught us how to put a cat in a carrier, regardless of whether they were hesitant or unfamiliar with it. According to McNee, the first step toward stress-free carrier interactions is early and frequent positive association.

When there are no upcoming trips planned for them, McNee suggests "start training your cat to love its carrier." Some cats may undergo the procedure quickly, while others may take longer. If you don't have a set amount of time, it will be easier for you to complete the steps at a pace that your cat is used to. McNee provides a step-by-step guide to all things cat carriers, from selecting the best carrier to putting your cat in it.

## Comforting your cat in their carrier:

Before your cat can become accustomed to using a carrier, you must find a way for her to enjoy her own space, as is the case with many desensitization training methods. McNee suggests starting with a clean slate—in this case, the carrier—if your cat had a bad experience there. You can get rid of any stress or fear hormones released by your cat by wiping down the carrier. After that, according to McNee, you can begin establishing a positive connection with your cat's carrier by utilizing a few of her favorite things: food, activities, and a cozy spot to nap The first step is for her carrier to become a part of her familiar surroundings. As a result, keep a warm blanket inside and keep the outside one outside. Start by removing the top for cats who are already apprehensive about cats in carriers.

We all know that cats love to eat, so the best way to connect with your cat is to feed her breakfast in her carrier. Serve meals close to the carrier's door at first, bringing her dish in daily.

During mealtimes, keep an eye out for and around the transporter for recess, and reward your cat whenever she chooses to connect with it.

It is best not to rush the process because the amount of time it takes for a cat to get used to her crate varies from cat to cat. Move on to closing the door of the carrier while your cat is inside once she gets used to it.

Gradually increase the duration until you can pick up the carrier, close the door, and walk around the house while your cat remains calm. Don't forget to treat her and give her verbal praise!

## How to get a Cat in a career

Your cat might be willing to enter with a little coaxing or a treat if she got used to her carrier well. If something goes wrong, McNee walks us through a straightforward two-step procedure.

Step 1. Get yourself and your cat ready

There are two ways to put your cat in her carrier: Before you pick up your cat, you should decide whether she will enter head first or bum first. Although both are acceptable, McNee suggests that bum first might be preferable for anxious cats. In the event of a headfirst fall, open the front door of the carrier. For the bum, open the top first. "McNee continues, "Prepare to move quickly, confidently, and smoothly in either direction."

If you have an anxious cat who is prone to running when she sees the carrier, place the carrier well in advance of any travel in a room with a door and limited hiding spots, such as your bathroom. Additionally, you should administer any unpleasant movement-promoting over-the-counter or prescription medication to your agitated cat prior to placing her in the transporter. Spraying Feliway on the blanket in the carrier or in your car can also help calm your cat.

## Step 2. Put the cat in the bag

"To ensure your cat's safety, pick it up with both hands;" The procedure is described as follows by McNee: Place one hand on their chest under their front legs and point your fingers in the direction of their chin while supporting their back with the other hand." If your cat likes to hide under blankets, covering the carrier with a blanket or towel can help her relax. Some people may feel more at ease when they have a clear view of their surroundings.

## Reasons Why Kittens Misbehave

In order to effectively put an end to kitten misbehavior, it is essential to comprehend the underlying causes. Cat misbehavior is frequently caused by the following things:

1.Boredom: Because they are naturally curious and active, kittens require a lot of mental and physical stimulation. They might start acting out in an effort to get attention or find something to do if they are bored.

**2. Inadequate preparation:** Cats must be taught from a young age what is and is not acceptable behavior. They might not know the difference between right and wrong if they haven't been trained.

**3. dread or anxiety:** A kitten may hide, scratch furniture, or even bite or scratch their owners if they are afraid or anxious.

**4. Teething:** During the teething phase, kittens must chew and bite to alleviate the discomfort caused by their new teeth.

## Kitten Misbehavior Solutions

Despite their adorable playfulness, kittens can also be naughty and behave badly. The following are some common feline misbehaviors that can be addressed:

**(1) Scratches on furniture:** Since kittens love to scratch furniture, it's important to keep them away. Reward your kitten for using a scratching post and ensure that they have access to one. You can also stop them from scratching the furniture by using things like aluminum foil or double-sided tape.

**(2) Jumping backwards:** If your kitten likes to jump on counters or other surfaces they shouldn't, create a designated area for them to climb and play in. Additionally, you can deter them from jumping on the counter by employing motion-activated spray or sticky mats.

**(3) Biting and scratching:** Even though kittens like to play rough, it's important to teach them that biting and scratching other people isn't acceptable behavior. If your kitten scratches or bites you, say "no" loudly and stop playing with them right away. You can also give them toys and play time to help them focus.

(4) A lot of meowing: If your kitten meows frequently, it could indicate that they need your attention, that they are thirsty, or that they are hungry. It's important to spend quality time with them every day and make sure they have food, water, and a clean litter box.

(5) Twisting Cords and Wires: Kittens may attempt to chew on wires and cords, which can be harmful, out of curiosity. To prevent this, cover wires and cords with cord protectors or keep them out of reach. Keep in mind that kittens are still learning and need patience as well as positive reinforcement to learn how to behave appropriately. By providing them with a stimulating and secure environment, you can assist them in developing into content cats with good manners.

6. Stop playing as soon as possible and ignore behaviors like biting or scratching:

Make it a point to teach your cat that it is unacceptable for them to bite or scratch you on a regular basis and become overly aggressive, as opposed to just occasionally biting you accidentally!

You should immediately stop playing with your cat or whining when this behavior occurs. Don't fuss or give your pet any attention; move out of their attack range and out of their way. The best way to stop aggressive play is to walk away from your pet, ignore them, and leave them alone for five to ten minutes without speaking to or looking in their direction. Do this every time your pet acts aggressively, and they will quickly learn that if they act badly, they will be ignored!

Because they are still in the learning stage of their development, it is best to teach this to your cat while they are still kittens. The best candidates for this strategy are adorable kittens and adult cats, both of which will crave your attention. Cats respond well to positive reinforcement, so keep your cool and be patient at all times.

## Chapter 2

## Raising Kittens Without a Mother

Raising a litter of orphaned kittens can be very difficult, but it can also be very rewarding. It is possible for kittens to become orphans for a variety of reasons, including the mother's death during childbirth or a sudden tragedy. Because kittens are so dependent on their mother for food, warmth, protection, and feces, trying to replace what they have lost can be very taxing. You might need to delegate some of your responsibilities to other people because you will only be spending the majority of your time with the kittens.

## Eight Simple Steps to Litter Train a Kitten Without a Mother

Starting at four weeks of age, this is how to begin litter training a kitten without their mother.

1. The cat's access is restricted:
You should initially restrict the kitten's space because they will begin this process so early. It's time to get started now that you've set them up in a comfortable room in a controlled area.

2. Place the Cat in the Litter Box Once More:
You should frequently demonstrate how to use the litter box when introducing the kitten to it. It's time to put them in the box when you notice them looking like they're looking for something, or when you know they just ate or woke up.

3. Digging with the Cat's Paw:
You can teach the kitten to dig because cats typically cover their waste on their own. As if they were covering, they gently dig their paws into the litter. They usually see mothers doing this, but you take their place as a human because it's impossible.

4. Give the kitten time to adjust to its new surroundings:
Additionally, the kitten ought to be permitted to adjust to the box on their own terms. They are able to get in and out, feel the things, and look around.

5. After each cleaning, put the trash in the trash can:
Always leave some waste in the litter box after each scoop. The kitten is able to associate this area with the need to pee because it can smell their vomit or poop.

The Hepper Advanced Bio-Enzyme Pet Stain & Odor Eliminator Spray can permanently remove even the worst pet stains and odors, even if you clean the litter box.

6. Give more access to the house over time:

You can gradually give your kitten access to more of the house once you believe they understand the concept. Allow them to roam the room if they are in a kennel. You can let them into additional areas until the entire area is open for play once they have mastered that.

7. Even after the cat has eaten or taken a nap, keep reminding it:

Your kitten may require more frequent reminders to use the bathroom the more freedom they have. Show them the litter box once more as a friendly reminder when they get up from a wonderful nap or just finished eating.

8. Utilize a number of urinals:

Numerous litter boxes should be provided once they understand the idea. If your house is big, even if your cat likes the idea of using the pan as a urinal, they might forget where it is.

## The best kitten food

Cats require specialized care and attention for social and physical development. Feeding them the right food is just as important as behavioral training. If a kitten eats well, its brain and body will develop more quickly. Many kitten-specific cat foods have ingredients that are higher in fat and calories to meet your kitten's nutritional needs.

We have compiled a list of our top picks to assist you in selecting the appropriate food for your cat. From the options listed below, you can select the type of kibble and wet food that is most suitable for your kitten.

## The Best Ten Cat Foods

Your cat's diet has a significant impact on its health. If your cat consumes a diet that does not satisfy all of its nutritional requirements, it may never be as healthy and vibrant. A healthy diet for cats is easy to talk about, but there's more to offer. Numerous manufacturers are producing high-quality commercial cat foods that can provide your pet with all of the necessary nutrients despite the fact that poor products make up a large portion of the pet market.

To determine which of these cat foods is best for our cats, we looked at a lot of ingredient lists and nutritional labels. Our top ten choices were as follows: You'll find out which three of them are worthy of our recommendations in the reviews that follow.

1. The Scientific Diet of Hill: This brand addresses hairball management, digestive health, and weight management, among other health issues.

2. Formulas made under the Royal Canin brand are well-known for catering to the particular requirements of various cat breeds.

3. Plan Pro Purina: This brand offers recipes for healthy urinary tracts and sensitive stomachs.

4. The buff Bill: Natural, grain-free formulas made with high-quality

ingredients and no poultry byproduct meal are available from this brand.

5.**Wellness**: High-protein, grain-free formulas made with real meat and free of artificial colors and preservatives are available from this brand.

6.**Orijen**: The formulas of this brand that are biologically appropriate are made with only fresh, local ingredients and no artificial additives.

7. **Surprised Taste**: Formulas made under this brand contain real roasted meats, probiotics, and other ingredients in addition to grains.

8.**Acana**: This brand makes formulas with regional flavors that don't contain any artificial colors or preservatives and are made with whole, fresh ingredients.

9.**Merrick**: A variety of grain-free, low-calorie formulas made with high-quality protein sources and no byproduct meal are available from this brand.

10.**Nutro**: With real meat as the primary ingredient and no artificial colors, flavors, or preservatives, this brand offers natural, grain-free formulas.

## Kitten litter training

Learning how to use the litter box is an essential part of early feline development, even though the term "litter training" can be a little misleading. Kittens will naturally understand and be compelled to use the litter box if you encourage them appropriately. Find out everything you need to know about leading kittens in the right direction.

## 1. Introduce Litter at the Right Time:

Because kittens don't use the litter box until they're about three weeks old, you need to get them to do so. When a kitten reaches the age of three weeks, it is appropriate to introduce them to the litter box. You should be patient with the kitten and keep stimulating her until you are certain that she uses the litter box consistently due to the fact that each kitten grows at a different rate.

## 2. Choose a litter that is suitable for cats:

Like humans, kittens learn and explore with their mouths. You will need to select a litter that is safe for your kittens to consume in order to ensure that they do not consume anything harmful or toxic. Products for cat litter should not have clumping properties, harsh chemicals, or scents. Even though adult cats frequently use clumping litter, kittens shouldn't be given it until they are at least two to three months old and accustomed to using the litter box. This is because if kittens ingest it, it could be harmful to them.

Choose a natural pellet-based litter instead, as young kittens are less likely to swallow or inhale it.

## 3. Choose the Right Box:

Cats require a shallow, open, and easy-to-find litter box with an open top. Remove obstacles like tall or covered boxes and provide something that is simple for them to enter and exit until they are large enough to use an adult litter box. Using a cardboard tray similar to those for canned kitten food, you can even provide a shallow lip for very young kittens under 8 weeks to walk over.

## 4. Choose the Best Placement:

The location is just as significant. Because kittens are known to gravitate toward corners and other locations that are not their primary residence, the litter box should be placed in a location that is free of clutter first. Placing a puppy pad beneath the box will make cleanup simpler because puppies can be messy learners.

When teaching a kitten to use a litter box, you should make it as simple as possible for them to locate it each time. Cats will instinctively choose the most convenient place to cover their waste. As a result, during their transition, you should keep them close to a box, and you should avoid providing the kitten with messy places like laundry piles because this could encourage bad habits. A kitten who is learning to use a litter box between the ages of 3 and 8 weeks should ideally be housed in a single room so that they can always find it. For older kittens who are adjusting to a larger space, it is best to offer multiple options so that the kitten is always within 10 feet of a litter box.

## 5. Utilize Positive Reward:

Cats benefit more from positive reinforcement than from punishment. Give kittens praise when they use the box correctly.

If the kitten uses it outside the box, clean and disinfect it immediately to prevent scent soaking or associations.

If the kitten is using the bedding and laundry, keep them off the ground. If a kitten frequents the area frequently, install a litter box there. Using a product like Kitten Attract or switching to a different litter can help a kitten that is having trouble understanding the box.

## 6. Tidy it up:

Not only do cats not want to use a filthy bathroom, either! Clean the box throughout the day at least once per day to encourage them to keep developing healthy habits. They will continue to use the bathroom when they need to when they have a tidy box, which is better for both of you and them.

# Three trucks to Teach your cat

## 1. Fetch:

- To teach your cat to fetch, put water in a tuna can and throw her favorite toy just out of reach. This will make use of their inherent hunting skills.
- Click and reward your cat whenever it walks toward the toy or picks it up. Keep your patience up; Your cat may need several sessions to grasp the concept.
- Click and give your cat a treat if it carries the toy toward you. After that, your cat will consume the treat and release the toy. You can add the cue word "fetch" to each throw once they consistently retrieve the toy.

## 2. Sit:

- If you're sitting on the floor, your cat won't be able to see you holding a clicker and a treat. After that, call your cat to you.
- Hold the treat a little bit higher than your cat's head. A cat will naturally sit as long as their eyes are following the treat. The reward comes before the "click."
- Reward only one position as your cat becomes more adept at sitting. You can begin using the cue word "sit" with your pet when he or she sits consistently nine times out of ten.

3. High-five:
- Call your cat back to you and give them something valuable, like a piece of chicken, as a reward.
- After that, you can start encouraging your cat to reach for the treat by using his natural "paw" movement. The best way to get your cat to reach up with their paws is to hold the chicken piece up to their nose. A command word like "tap" and praise and a reward should be part of their response.
- If you play this game with your cat every day as a fun activity, you will soon be able to ask for a high five.

# The Characteristics of the House Cat:

Not only is it important to teach a cat the word "no" to protect your furniture from the cat's razor-sharp nails, but you should also teach a cat the word "no" if you notice your cat engaging in potentially dangerous or dangerous behaviors like chewing on poisonous houseplants or climbing on windowsills or rafters.

The best first-time cat owner advice is frequently teaching a cat the meaning of the word "no" and consistently following through on it. A kitten will need to learn a lot during their first few months in your home, one of the most important of which is the meaning of the word "no."

You can focus on curbing undesirable behaviors before they become ingrained after a kitten has been litter-trained and adjusted to their new environment. A kitten will chew, scratch, and go where they shouldn't, coming up with creative and amusing ways to get into trouble.

## Why do cats claw at furniture?

Your cat must learn which areas of the house are off limits and what behaviors are acceptable during this time. Any actions that could be harmful to the cat or your property should be discouraged. To prevent your new cat from repeatedly scratching the same area, for instance, if your cat begins to claw at furniture, you must immediately discourage this behavior. Redirect them to an appropriate spot for scratching and insistently decline.

A cat's nails can become dangerously long and snag on furniture and clothing if they are not filed down correctly. If you say no to your cat, they must have a safe place to scratch; If not, they will pick a new location on their own.

Scratching posts on cat trees like the Kitty Mansions Cat Tree allow your cat to file their nails and provide a suitable location for your cat to play and climb. Find out more about five of the best models and what you should look for in a new cat tree by reading our buyer's guide to cat trees.

## Teaching No to your cat

When used to stop unsafe or undesirable behavior, the word "no" is easy for your cat to understand when spoken repeatedly and loudly. That word should be taught to your cat to denote actions or destinations they should avoid. Remember that you won't get the results you want right away by simply saying no. Your cat must first be instructed to stop doing things right away.

For instance, the time to act is now if your cat starts scratching the sofa in the living room or climbing the curtains. Say "no!" in a loud, firm voice. Pick up the cat and say "no" twice or three times as the next step. Move the cat to their cat tree or another secure spot where it can scratch.

As was mentioned earlier, a cat's scratching behavior is completely normal and allows the cat to polish, file, and clean its claws. Place the cat tree where the cat has been scratching, such as next to the couch, so that the preferred option is easily visible.

Each time you notice the cat scratching the curtains or furniture, you will be responsible for repeating this procedure. If you ignore this behavior, you are not establishing the boundaries your cat needs to learn what is and is not acceptable. When you say no to your cat, make sure you don't sound angry or violent. Be firm. The cat will only be scared if you act irate. A whole new set of undesirable behaviors, such as excessive meowing, grooming, and even spraying, may be displayed by anxious cats.

Chapter 3

# How to toilet train a kitten in seven easy steps

Because kittens are extremely intelligent animals, you should be able to fully train them in no time if you begin toilet training them immediately. If you want to ensure that your kitten's toilet training goes off without a hitch, you need to follow these seven crucial steps.

## First Step:

Your cat's poop is right next to the bathroom. Keep the litter box where you think is easiest for your cat to use for as long as it takes for them to get used to it.

**Pro-Tip:** Slow down. If your cat gets lost, it might look for a safe place to "go" in your home. After a few of these mishaps, it might be hard to break this bad habit. Instead, when deciding when to proceed, pay attention to your pet's behavior.

## Second Step:

Gradually raise the litter box's height. Remove a small amount each time you raise the height of the litter box. **Pro-Tip**: To ensure that it does not move when your cat jumps on it, secure the litter box to a stack of phone books or newspapers.

### Third Step:

Each day, move the litter box closer to the bathroom to ensure that it is directly above the seat. It is recommended that the litter be removed from the case on a regular basis until it has been reduced to a fine layer no deeper than an inch.

### Fourth Step:

Install a "training box" in place of your litter box. Check to see if the training box can hold your cat's weight. At this location, you have several options. You can make your own or buy one from a business.

The following are step-by-step instructions for making your own preparation box:

- A piece of wax paper should be taped to the entire seat of the toilet after it has been raised.
- Litter ought to be contained in the flushable wax paper as well.
- An aluminum pan or bowl can be used to tape the toilet seat's edges. Place the pan on the toilet seat to keep it in place. Litter that can be flushed can be stored in the pan.

**Pro-Tip:** After each use, empty the litter and add some catnip to the clean litter.

## Step 5:

Change your cat's behavior so she always uses the bathroom. Make a hole about an inch in diameter in the center of the aluminum or wax paper pan and gradually increase its size until the cover is almost gone. Reduce the size of the cover and the amount of litter in order to eliminate litter when the paper or bowl is removed.

## Sixth Step:

After every time your cat uses the toilet, flush it.

**Pro-Tip:** Never instruct your cat to relieve herself. Although cats have the ability to learn to flush, they occasionally overindulge and waste water.

## Seventh Step:

Feed your pet some food! It is essential to your cat's success to give them a reward when they perform well.

**Pro-Tip:** Add some litter to the bowl if your cat is afraid of the water; Your cat will associate the scent with his litter box.

Is it normal for your cat to urinate? If not, when do you intend to instruct them?

# Toilet training your cat may present seven challenges

Naturallythere are a few kits and numerous adorable or funny videos of cats using the bathroom. Therefore, teaching your cat how to "go to the bathroom" may appear "natural" or tempting. Especially if you live in a small apartment, don't want to clean a litter box, or just find the idea of a cat perched above the bowl funny. However, regardless of your motivations, there are a number of significant reasons not to toilet train your cat that you really ought to take into consideration first.

## 1. Consolidating the Data

A change in your cat's urine volume or frequency could be caused by more than just a urinary tract infection. A partial list of conditions that can alter the quantity or frequency of urine is as follows:

1. Diabetes
2. hyperthyroidism
3. kidney problems
4. bladder inflammation, also known as cystitis
5. dehydration
6. obstruction of the urethra, which can cause death quickly!

Early diagnosis and treatment, like those for many other medical conditions, can lessen your cat's suffering, make management simpler, and save you money. Consequently, you can't ignore these changes.

Even if your cat urinates in a toilet bowl, you won't be able to tell when it changes volume or frequency. On the other hand, cats who use litter boxes show these changes immediately. Are the clumps of poop different in size from usual? Are the clumps of pee bigger or smaller than usual? Every time you scoop the litter boxes, your cat's endocrine and urinary systems will give you an "update." This is not the case when a cat pees in a toilet!

## 2. Insane Toxo

28

Toxoplasmosis, another name for the parasite Toxoplasma gondii, is a disease. Do you know anything about it? Toxo")? Cats have a chance of contracting toxo, a nasty parasite, if they consume a mouse, rat, bird, or other wild animal. Cats that only reside inside are less likely to contract Toxo, despite the fact that rats and mice are pretty good at breaking into homes.)

All of the infected cats will shed infectious Toxoplasma oocysts in their feces for some time, despite the fact that not all of them will exhibit symptoms of the disease. Additionally, the typical wastewater treatments that are applied to flushed water cannot eradicate these infectious oocysts. This suggests that the disease and parasite it spreads may end up in nearby lakes, rivers, streams, and other water bodies, where they may infect otters, seals, and other aquatic animals. The Toxo oocyst contamination can also pose a threat to you and the other members of your household if your cat ever "misses" and drops a bomb on the toilet seat!

## 3. The lid or the cat either fall off

You can teach them to "do their business" by placing a cat perched on the edge of a toilet bowl. Even cats, on the other hand, have a limited range of motion. You will need to ensure that the top lid is always open and the bottom lid is always down if you want to let the cat "go" into the bathroom. The cat will have a place to perch here. Keep in mind that Mr. Jinx from Meet the Parents lacked the strength to lift a toilet seat and had opposable thumbs.

Your cat will find other places to urinate, such as your bed, shoes, carpet, or potted plants, if the top lid is left down because it can't use the toilet. Your cat will almost certainly fall into the seat if it is left up! Even if a cat has a perch, it is still easy for them to fall into the toilet, and the thought of having to deal with a cat covered in toilet water should be reason enough not to teach a cat how to use the bathroom!

## 4. Access is required

If your cat knows how to go to the bathroom, it needs to leave right away! What do you think your cat will do when you, another member of your family, or even a houseguest already hold the throne? Or what if someone left the door open when they left, but nobody is using the bathroom at the moment? They might have forgotten that your cat also uses the people's toilet or that you ran out of air freshener in your bathroom. What will your cat do in either scenario? Unfortunately, the typical response will be either that they will become overwhelmed or that they will look for a safe haven somewhere else, like your bed, the carpets, or the laundry. You just have to leave someday, you know!

## 5. When Jumping Hurts

Every time your cat needs to use the bathroom, they should have to walk a significant distance unless you build an incline or flight of stairs. However, what should you do if your cat is unable to jump, such as following surgery? Also, if your cat develops painful arthritis and cannot jump, what will happen? Did you know that over 90% of cats over the age of 12 and 30% of cats over the age of 8 suffer from arthritis? The prevalence of arthritis in cats is surprising!

Therefore, there is a good chance that your cat will develop arthritis in the future, even if they do not currently have the condition. After that, you'll have to teach your cat to use a litter box instead of the toilet, especially one with lower sides.

Your cat will find another place to go if they have to jump onto the toilet to go pee or poo and either gets hurt or is unable to do so.

## 6. that goes against their beliefs

Because cats naturally cover their waste, we continue to use litter. In the wild, this is an important way to cover up the smell and avoid predators.

Your cat still needs to put things in the ground, even though they don't live in the wild. If you just listen the next time your cat uses the litter box, you can still hear them scratching and burying their waste even if you are across the hall.

If you replace their litter with a toilet, they won't be able to bury themselves, but neither will their instinct or desire. Cats continue to exhibit this instinctive behavior by pawing at the area around them even after being toilet-trained. However, if they are unable to bury their waste, they may experience additional stress, which may result in a fall while using the bathroom or other stress-related issues.

## 7. Kitty won't be able to make it

31

You should ask your loved ones if they would mind using the bathroom with you if you want to take your toilet-trained cat on a trip, such as to your house for the holidays or to spend time with friends. That might be a problem that makes everyone feel uneasy if that is not the case when you get there. And even if they are in agreement, do you believe that they will always remember to keep the lid open, or do you believe that your cat will have its own bathroom?

Also, what will happen to your cat if he gets sick and needs to be boarded or taken to the vet? Expect significant issues if your toilet-trained cat is not also trained and accustomed to using a litter box.

# How to train a kitten to sleep at night

The general guidelines that follow can assist you in getting a better night's sleep and improve your cat's behavior at night:

**1. Establish a routine:** Cats are creatures of habit and thrive in routine. If you establish a consistent bedtime routine for your cat, such as feeding and playing with them before bed, they will learn to associate nighttime with sleep and quiet.

**2. Provide a cozy sleeping environment:** Cats need a warm, inviting spot to sleep where they can feel safe. Make sure your cat has a designated place to sleep and a cozy bed or blanket.

**3. Recognize yourself:** Positive reinforcement can be used to train your cat to behave in a certain way. Reward your cat with treats or praise when they behave well at night, like staying off your bed.

## 4. Create a separate sleeping space:
If your cat insists on sleeping on your bed and wakes you up, create a separate area for them to sleep. Provide a comfortable bed and some toys in a quiet area of your bedroom, like a corner or under a table.

## 5. Maintain distance:
Ensure that your cat gets plenty of playtime and exercise during the day to increase their chances of falling asleep at night. Play with your cat for at least 20 to 30 minutes before going to bed to tire them out.

## 6. Employ dissuasion:
If your cat continues to wake you up, use deterrents like double-sided tape, aluminum foil, or a motion-activated air canister to stop them from jumping on your bed at night.

Remember that patience and persistence are required when training your cat. With time and persistence, your cat will eventually learn to respect your sleep and allow you to get a good night's sleep.

## Conclusion

Cat training can be beneficial for both you and your feline companions. Successful training requires an understanding of your cats' behaviors, motivations, and limitations.

Your cat will benefit from training because it strengthens their bond with you and provides them with the necessary social and environmental enrichment. They can stay out of

trouble and lead happy, healthy lives
by avoiding boredom.

Printed in Great Britain
by Amazon

44348066R00020